King of the Knock-Knock Jokes

By Lael Littke

Illustrated by Peter Stevenson

DOMINIE PRESS

Pearson Learning Group

Publisher: Raymond Yuen
Project Editor: John S. F. Graham
Editor: Bob Rowland
Designer: Greg DiGenti
Illustrator: Peter Stevenson

Published by:

ṗ Dominie Press, Inc.

1949 Kellogg Avenue
Carlsbad, California 92008 USA

www.dominie.com

1-800-232-4570

Paperback ISBN 0-7685-2063-0
Printed in Singapore
  3 4 5 6   10 09 08 07 06

Table of Contents

Chapter One
The Most Popular Kid in School

My best friend, Tad, decided to call himself "The King of the Knock-Knock Jokes." He said people like someone who can make them laugh. He said he'll be the most popular kid in school, and when he grows up he'll be so popular that he'll run for president of the United States.

I said he was just going to get into trouble.

For a while things worked out all right. But then last week a new girl came into our class. Her name is Emma. Tad went up to her on the playground at recess and said, "Knock, knock."

"Huh?" said Emma.

"You're supposed to say, 'Who's there?' " Tad told her.

"Who's there?" Emma asked.

"Emma," Tad said.

Emma made her eyes into little slits and scowled down at Tad. She's taller than he is. "Are you trying to be funny?" she said. "Emma is *my* name."

Tad sighed. "I know it's *your* name. You're supposed to say, 'Emma who?' "

"Why?" asked Emma.

Tad sighed louder. "Not 'why.' Say 'Emma who?' "

Emma rolled her eyes. "OK," she said. "Emma who?"

Tad grinned. "Emma going to have trouble with you?"

The kids who were nearby laughed, but Emma put her hands on her hips. "Are you making fun of me, you little twerp?"

Tad's grin faded away. "Hey, it was just a joke." He backed away and came to stand by me. "Can you believe her, Eddie?"

"Tad," I said, "you'd better cool it with the jokes."

"Never," Tad said. "You wait and see. My jokes are going to make me popular."

Chapter Two
Mrs. Jewel Conway

The next day we had a new teacher because Mrs. Olson left to have a baby. Our new teacher wrote her name on the chalkboard: Mrs. Jewel Conway.

Tad put up his hand.

Mrs. Conway consulted a seating

chart and said, "Tad? Do you have something to say?"

Tad smiled at her. "Knock, knock," he said.

Mrs. Conway smiled, too. "Who's there?"

"Jewel," Tad said.

I frowned to signal Tad to lay off that kind of stuff with a teacher. But he didn't pay any attention.

"Jewel who?" Mrs. Conway said.

"Jewel soon get to know who we all are," Tad said.

Mrs. Conway laughed, and so did most of the kids. They stomped their feet and reached out to give Tad high-fives. Except Emma. And me. I was too worried that Tad was going to get into trouble.

"That's very funny, Tad," Mrs. Conway said. "Thank you for starting off my day here with a laugh."

Emma raised her hand. "It just sounds dumb to me."

Mrs. Conway looked at the seating chart again. "It's just a knock-knock joke, Emma," she said. "Some people think they are funny."

"Well, I don't," Emma said. She scowled at Tad.

"Let's get on to our work," Mrs. Conway said. "Open your social studies books. I understand you've been learning about Alaska and the Yukon Territory."

Tad's hand shot up again. "Knock, knock," he said.

Mrs. Conway didn't smile this time, but she said, "Who's there?"

"Yukon."

"Yukon who?" Mrs. Conway said.

"Yukon call on me anytime you want," Tad said.

Everybody laughed again, except Emma and me. Emma pointed a finger down her throat to show that the joke made her sick.

Mrs. Conway didn't say anything. She looked at Tad for so long that I was sure she was going to send him out of the room.

Chapter Three

The Capital of Alaska

Mrs. Conway, our new teacher, didn't laugh after Tad told the second knock-knock joke. She did finally smile a little and say, "Tad, I really like knock-knock jokes, and it's always good to laugh. But it's time to get on with our lesson, OK?"

"OK," Tad said. "I'm sorry, Mrs. Conway."

I breathed a sigh of relief because I didn't want Tad to get into trouble.

Mrs. Conway was back in control again. "All right, class," she said, "who can tell me the capital of Alaska?"

Tad's hand was the first one up.

"Tad?" said Mrs. Conway.

Tad hesitated. Oh, no. He wasn't going to do another knock-knock joke, was he?

He looked over at me. I rolled my eyes, trying to tell him to forget it.

He looked back at Mrs. Conway. "Knock, knock," he said.

She stared at him, not saying anything.

Emma was hanging on to her desk as if she might fall right off her chair.

Finally Robert yelled out from the

other side of the room, "Who's there?"

"Juneau," Tad said.

"Juneau who?" Robert yelled.

"Juneau the capital of Alaska?" Tad said. As the class laughed and stomped and hollered, he stood up and took a bow.

Emma leaped to her feet. "What's so funny about that."

Tad stared up at her. "You wouldn't know funny if it hopped up and bit you."

Emma slammed her fists onto her hips. "Oh, yeah? Why don't you crawl back into the woodwork, you little termite? Why don't you leave your brain to science—maybe they could find a cure for it!"

By now the whole class was in an uproar, laughing and stomping and high-fiving all over the place.

But Mrs. Conway wasn't laughing. Not a bit.

Chapter Four
Mr. Kent

Mrs. Conway didn't look very happy. I wasn't sure who was in trouble.

Was it Tad? Was it Emma? Or was it our whole class?

Before Mrs. Conway could say

anything, there was a knock on our door.

Mrs. Conway kept a stern eye on all of us as she opened it.

Our principal, Mr. Kent, came in.

"I thought I'd come help the class welcome you to our school, Mrs. Conway," he said with a big smile. He gazed around at all of us, and then at Mrs. Conway. His smile faded. "Is there a problem?"

Mrs. Conway's eyes swept up and down each row. "Is there a problem, class?"

Nobody said anything. We were all a little afraid of Mr. Kent. He was very tall and had big shoulders. He could squash any of us if he wanted to.

Finally Tad put up his hand.

Mrs. Conway didn't seem to want to see it, so finally Mr. Kent said, "Tad?"

"Knock, knock," Tad said in a small voice.

Mrs. Conway frowned, but Mr. Kent said, "Who's there?"

"Kent." Tad's voice shrank to a squeak.

Mr. Kent looked at him for a moment and said, "Kent who?"

Tad gulped and said, "Kent you tell how smart we are?"

Mr. Kent looked at him for a moment before he said, "You like knock-knock jokes, don't you, Tad?"

Tad nodded. "Yes. And that's the problem."

I was proud of Tad for confessing. But now he was definitely in trouble.

Before even thinking, I blurted, "I like tongue twisters best. Like 'Six thick thistle sticks.' Say it fast three times."

Now Mr. Kent looked at me. So did Mrs. Conway. So did Emma and the rest of our class.

I was in trouble now, too.

Chapter Five
Tad's All, Folks!

Our classroom was silent.

Finally Emma said, "They're both just what the doctor ordered—pills."

Mr. Kent shifted his gaze to her. "Hmm," he said thoughtfully. "Tad likes knock-knock jokes, Eddie likes tongue twisters, and Emma likes insults." He cleared his throat while we all slid down in our seats. "As for me," he said, "I like riddles. Why is a schoolyard larger at recess than it is during class time?"

We all thought about it, but nobody could guess.

"Because at recess there are more feet in it," Mr. Kent said, smiling.

We all laughed.

Suddenly Mrs. Conway smiled, too. "I like monster mix-ups," she said.

I raised my hand. "Tell us one, please."

"OK," said Mrs. Conway. "What do you get if you cross Bambi with a ghost?"

The whole class said, "What?"

"Bamboo!" Mrs. Conway said.

Everybody laughed at her joke, too. Even Emma.

Suddenly I had an idea. I raised my hand again. "We all like different kinds of funny stuff. Why don't we do a show for the rest of the school about what makes people laugh?"

"That's a great idea, Eddie," said Mrs. Conway. "What do you think, Mr. Kent?"

"I think we should put Eddie and Tad in charge of it," Mr. Kent said. "How about it, boys?"

"Sure," I said.

"Knock, knock," Tad said.

"Who's there?" we all said.

"Eddie."

"Eddie who?"

"Eddie body else want to help?" Tad said.

While everybody laughed again, Tad leaned over to me. "Thanks for saving me, Eddie," he whispered. "When I get to

be president of the United States, I'll let you be my vice president."

We high-fived.

"You boys can start planning the program at lunchtime," Mr. Kent said. "It's time to work now." He walked toward the door and stopped. "Knock, knock," he said.

"Who's there?" we asked.

"Tad," he said.

"Tad who?"

"Tad's all, folks," Mr. Kent said as he went out.